AIR
experimenting with science

Antonella Meiani

Lerner Publications Company · Minneapolis

First American edition published in 2003 by Lerner Publications Company

Published by arrangement with Istituto Geografico DeAgostini, Novara, Italy

Originally published as *Il Grande Libro degli Esperimenti*

Copyright © 1999 by Istituto Geografico DeAgostini, Novara, Italy

Translated from the Italian by Maureen Spurgeon.
Translation copyright © 2000 by Brown Watson, England.

This book has been adapted from a single-volume work entitled *Il Grande Libro degli Esperimenti,* originally published by Istituto Geografico DeAgostini, Novara, Italy, in 1999. New back matter was developed by Lerner Publications Company.

Lerner Publications Company
A division of Lerner Publishing Group
241 First Avenue North
Minneapolis, MN 55401 U.S.A.

Website address: www.lernerbooks.com

Library of Congress Cataloging-in-Publication Data

Meiani, Antonella.
   [Il Grande libro degli esperimenti. English. Selections]
   Air / by Antonella Meiani ; [translated from the Italian by Maureen Spurgeon]
  1st American ed.
     p.   cm. — (Experimenting with science)
   Includes bibliographical references and index.
   Summary: Explains the properties of air through experiments which feature such topics as what air is, how much force wind has, what shape is best for flying, and how sound travels.
   ISBN: 0–8225–0082–5 (lib. bdg. : alk. paper)
   1. Air—Experiments—Juvenile literature. [1. Air—Experiments. 2. Experiments.]
  I. Title.
QC161.2.M4513   2003
533'.6'078—dc21   2001037730

Manufactured in the United States of America
1 2 3 4 5 6 – JR – 08 07 06 05 04 03

Table of Contents

Air

What is air? Does air weigh anything? Can it exert any force? How much force does the wind have? What shape is best for flying? How do sounds travel?

You will find the answers to these and many other questions by doing the experiments in the following pages, under the following headings:

- Air is everywhere
- Air pressure
- Hot and cold air
- Flight
- Air and combustion
- Sounds

Air is everywhere

Air is everywhere, taking up every free space. There is air in water, objects, plants, animals, and even the human body. Although air is light and invisible, we can still find ways to weigh and see it.

Where can we find air?

IN WATER WITHOUT GETTING WET

You need:
- clear glass jar
- table-tennis ball
- paper towel
- transparent bowl or basin (deeper than the jar) containing water

What to do:

1 Push the paper towel into the bottom of the jar so that it cannot move around.

2 Place the table-tennis ball on the surface of the water in the bowl.

3 Turn the jar upside-down over the table-tennis ball. Press down with the jar until it touches the bottom of the bowl.

What happens?
The water does not get into the jar, and the table-tennis ball is resting on the bottom of the bowl, almost dry.

Why?
The air in the jar keeps the water from getting in. Lift the jar straight up out of the water and you will see that the paper towel is dry or only barely wet.

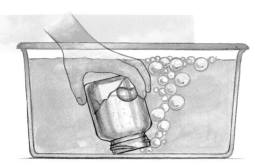

4 Immerse the jar once again.

5 When the jar touches the bottom, tilt it a little.

What happens?
Bubbles of air escape from the jar. They rise to the surface and burst. Water gets into the jar, the ball rises higher inside, and the paper towel gets wet.

Why?
The air inside the jar finds a way to escape and rises upward. Now water takes up the space that the air once filled.

Vacuum-packed products

If you read the information printed on jars of coffee, you may see the words *vacuum packed*. This term refers to a special manufacturing process that removes the air inside the jar so that the coffee is better preserved. When the seal is opened, you can hear a noise that is almost like a breath. This is the air taking up space again inside the jar.

Air in water

Water contains air too. You can see that by leaving a glass full of water near a source of heat. When the water begins to warm up, you will notice tiny bubbles full of air collecting together on the inside of the glass.

But human beings cannot breathe the air in water. Under water we have to use a snorkel to take air from the surface or breathe from tanks full of oxygen.

Air is all around. It occupies every free space, however small.

Does air have weight?

You need:
- two drinking straws, one cut to 15 cm (6 in.)
- two balloons of equal size, each slightly inflated
- two soda cans
- tape
- pencil

What to do:

1 Mark the center of the long straw with the pencil.

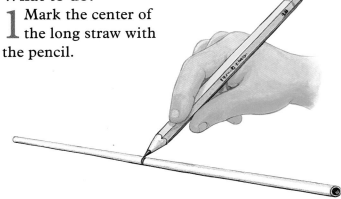

2 Tape one balloon to each end of the long straw.

3 Tape each end of the short straw to a soda can. Place the center mark of the long straw on top of the short straw.

What happens?
The stick with the two balloons stays horizontal.

Why?
The balloons are of equal weight.

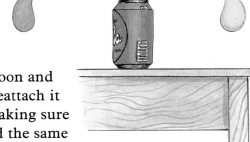

4 Remove one balloon and inflate it fully. Reattach it to the long straw, making sure the straw is centered the same as before.

What happens?
The fully inflated balloon weighs down one end of the long straw.

Why?
The air inside the fully inflated balloon makes it heavier than the other balloon.

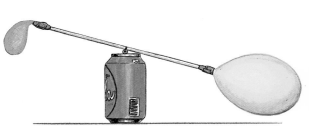

THE AIR IN A ROOM

You need:
- tape measure
- pen and paper
- bathroom scales

What to do:

1 Take the measurement of a room in meters. (This is best done from corner to corner.) Measure the width and the length of the floor and the height of one wall.

2 Multiply the three measurements together to obtain the volume of the room in cubic meters (volume = width × length × height).

3 Scientists have calculated that one cubic meter of air weighs approximately 1.2 kg (2.6 lbs.). So if you multiply the volume of a room by 1.2, you will obtain the weight of the air in the room.

4 Now weigh yourself. Compare your own weight with that of the air in the room. Which is more?

What happens?
You will find that the air in the room weighs more than you do.

Why?
The air in a medium-sized room weighs as much as an adult person—about 70 kg (150 lbs.).

Bubbles of air to attract prey

A table-tennis ball released underwater springs up and breaks free. Then it spins rapidly on the surface, because it is lighter than the water on which it floats. That is why bubbles of air always rise through water.

The humpback whale uses this phenomenon (something happening naturally that we can see, feel, or hear) to capture its prey. The whale moves in circles below a school of fish, making air bubbles that rise up toward the surface of the water. These bubbles attract the fish toward the whale, who is waiting to swallow them up.

Even something that is as light as air has weight.

Air pressure

The atmosphere is a thick layer of air surrounding the earth (about 1,000 km [600 mi.] deep). It exerts its pressure on bodies and objects, but nobody is aware of it. Yet 15 metric tons (17 tons) of air presses down on a grown-up person! Although we cannot feel the great strength of air pressure on us, it is possible to measure it, increase it, and use it to operate machines and to overcome the force of gravity.

Does air exert a force?

AN INVISIBLE FORCE

You need:
- ruler
- large sheet of paper
- board to work on

What to do:

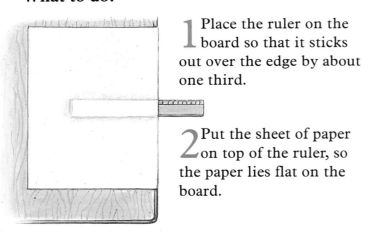

1 Place the ruler on the board so that it sticks out over the edge by about one third.

2 Put the sheet of paper on top of the ruler, so the paper lies flat on the board.

3 Hit the part of the ruler that is sticking out to try to make the paper jump up into the air. (Make sure the blow is not hard enough to break the ruler!)

What happens?
The paper keeps the ruler from lifting up.

Why?
Air is pressing down on the paper. Because the surface of the paper is large, the quantity of air on it is enough to keep the paper from rising, despite the force of the blow.

AIR MAKES WATER RISE

You need:
- large bowl or tub
- drinking glass
- water

What to do:

1 Put the glass into the bowl full of water and turn it upside-down.

2 Lift up the glass, but do not let the rim go above the surface of the water.

What happens?

The level of water in the glass rises so that it is higher than the water outside the glass.

Why?

The pressure of air on the surface of the water pushes the water up into the glass. If the rim of the glass were raised above the surface of the water, air would enter and push the water out. Then the glass would be empty.

Air exerts pressure on all surfaces with which it comes in contact.

Does air only press downward?

STRONGER THAN WATER

You need:
- glass with a smooth rim
- postcard or a piece of postcard-sized glossy cardboard
- water
- sink in which to work

What to do:

1 Fill the glass with water.

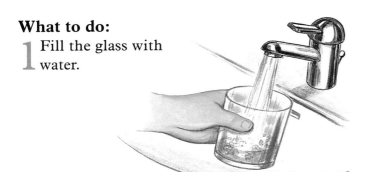

2 Carefully place the glossy side of the postcard down on the rim of the glass. (You will eventually make it a little wet.)

3 Keeping the palm of your hand on the card, turn the glass upside-down.

4 Take your hand away from the card.

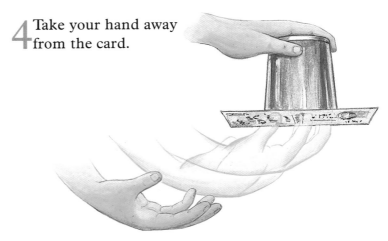

What happens?
The card remains attached to the rim of the glass and the water does not fall out.

Why?
The air pressure exerted on the card from underneath is greater than the weight of the water inside the glass. This is why the card holds the water so it does not spill out.

The power of suction
When a suction cup or plunger is pressed down on a surface, the air that is inside escapes. Because of the air pressure outside, the rubber of the suction cup stays firmly attached to the surface, completely airtight. But if you lift the edge of the rubber, air gets in and the suction cup no longer works because the air pressure inside and outside the cup is the same. You can prove this for yourself by testing which surfaces the suction cup will stick to and which it will not stick to.

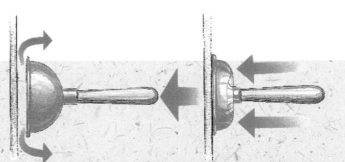

You will find that a suction cup will work only on perfectly smooth surfaces. On rough surfaces, the air presses down on the suction cup and immediately gets into any gap between the surface and the suction cup rubber.

Air pressure is exerted in all directions, including from the bottom to the top.

Does the air that surrounds Earth press down on us?

THE PRINTS

You need:
- modeling clay
- glass bottle full of water and sealed with a cork

What to do:
1 Soften the clay and mold it into a fairly thick, round base the same size as the base of the bottle.

2 Place the bottle on the clay base, taking care to keep it upright.

3 Remove the bottle. Turn it upside-down and put it on the clay base again.

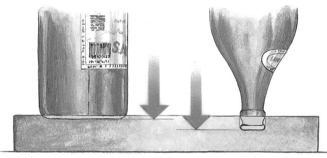

What happens?
The print left in the clay by the upright bottle is not as deep as the print left by the upside-down bottle.

Why?
The surface on which the weight of the upright bottle is distributed is larger. When the bottle is upside-down, the same weight is concentrated on a smaller surface. This exerts greater pressure, so the upside-down bottle leaves a much deeper print. The pressure exerted by a human body also depends on how large the surface of contact is. That is why skis prevent skiers from sinking into the snow!

A balance of strength
Atmospheric pressure is determined by the weight of the air above us, which presses down on everything found on the surface of Earth. How is it that it never crushes us? The human body has many different surfaces on which air pressure is distributed in different directions. And, most important, inside our bodies, as in the bodies of all animals, there is air that presses toward the outside to equal the atmospheric pressure. Due to this balance of forces, we can withstand the atmospheric pressure that pushes on us.

Variations in pressure
Atmospheric pressure in the mountains is less than atmospheric pressure at sea level. The higher you go, the thinner the layer of air that is above you. Therefore, less atmospheric pressure is exerted. The same applies under water. The deeper you go, the more you feel the weight of the water increasing. Atmospheric pressure also changes with temperature (hot air weighs less than cold air) and with humidity, or dampness. (Air that carries water vapor is heavier than dry air.) Because of these variations, we need to use instruments, such as barometers and altimeters, to measure atmospheric pressure.

A barometer is used to measure atmospheric pressure. It can predict changes in weather conditions.

The atmosphere presses down equally on bodies and objects. It is balanced by the pressure of air within them.

Can air be compressed?

SQUASH THE AIR

You need:
- plastic syringe without a needle

What to do:

1 Lift the plunger of the syringe so that the syringe fills with air.

2 Cover the hole of the syringe with a finger and press down hard on the plunger. Then let go of the plunger.

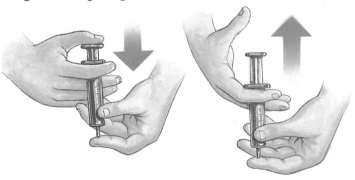

What happens?
The plunger shoots up and then stops. You feel a strong push against your finger. Take your finger away from the hole and the plunger returns to its original position.

Why?
The air is compressed because the plunger makes it occupy a much smaller space. This compression increases the air pressure inside the syringe, and that is the force with which the air presses against the inside of the syringe and on your finger. The plunger rises because the compressed air expands. The pressure drops when you remove your finger from the hole. If you repeat the experiment with a syringe full of water, you will find that the plunger does not shoot up.

The strength of compressed air

The compressed air inside a pneumatic tire is able to support the weight of a bicycle, car, or automatic train. The tire's flexible, springy surface cushions the vehicle when the wheels go over bumps or any unevenness in the ground.

Helicopters and parachutes work by making use of air pressure. As the rotor blade of a helicopter whirls, it pushes the air downward, compressing it and getting a force to help it take off and push up into the sky.

The shape of a parachute is designed to gather and compress under it a great quantity of air that presses upward. This is enough to counteract the force of falling and slow down the descent.

A hovercraft is a form of transportation that can move on ground and on water, suspended on a cushion of air.

Instruments as simple as an eyedropper and as complex as a jet engine work due to air pressure being compressed in a reduced space. You use compressed air each time you let go of an inflated balloon to see it fly through the air.

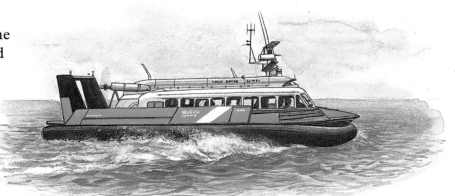

JET-PROPELLED BALLOONS

You need:
- string
- tape
- medium-sized balloon
- drinking straw

What to do:

1 Thread the string through the straw and tie the ends tightly between two points at equal height in a room (such as handles or hooks).

2 Inflate the balloon and keep the neck closed between your fingers.

3 Tape the balloon underneath the drinking straw and pull the balloon to one end of the string.

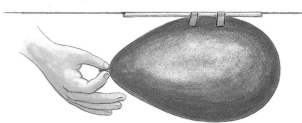

4 Let the balloon go.

What happens?
The balloon shoots along the string.

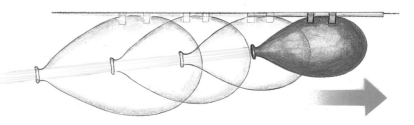

Why?
When the balloon is closed, the air inside presses evenly against the inside surface. When the balloon is let go, the air inside expands out of the mouth of the balloon. This creates a backward thrust, and the reaction is the balloon pushing forward.

The force of reaction

The arm strokes of a swimmer or the strokes from the oar of a rower show us how, for each force of action, there is a force of reaction. The push of the arm or oar on the water causes a push of equal strength in the opposite direction, which makes the swimmer or the rower move forward. This is how a jet aircraft works. Its engines shoot out bursts of very hot exhaust gases behind it, and the reaction to this is powerful enough to propel the aircraft forward.

Air can be compressed. The force of compressed air can support and move considerable weights.

Hot and cold air

Great masses of hot and cold air move around in the atmosphere. Weather satellites take photographs of these air masses for meteorologists to study so they can forecast rains and hurricanes. These masses of air constantly flow all around Earth, due to the heat of the Sun.

What happens to air that is heated?

HEATING AND COOLING AIR

You need:
- balloon
- empty bottle
- basin with hot water (Take care—hot water must be handled with caution!)

What to do:

1 Inflate the balloon slightly and place it on the neck of the bottle.

2 Hold the bottle in hot water for a minute or two.

What happens?
The balloon inflates.

Why?
The air, like all substances, is made up of tiny, moving particles called molecules. Heat makes these molecules move apart. This means that the air inside the bottle expands and needs more space. So it expands into the balloon and inflates it.

3 Run cold water on the bottle.

What happens?
The balloon deflates.

Why?
The air, now affected by the cold, contracts (the molecules come closer together). Once again the air occupies only the space in the bottle.

THE MAGIC GLASS

You need:
- drinking glass
- thick book
- board with a smooth surface
- cold water and hot water

What to do:

1 Balance the board on the book so it is slightly tilted. Rinse the glass in cold water and put it upside-down on the highest point of the board. Be ready to catch the glass so it doesn't fall!

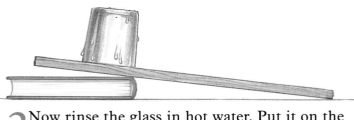

2 Now rinse the glass in hot water. Put it on the highest point of the board.

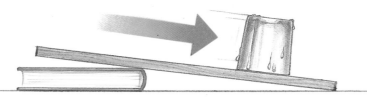

What happens?
When the glass is rinsed in cold water, it moves slowly toward the bottom of the board, then stops. When the glass is rinsed in hot water, it slides rapidly to the bottom.

Why?
The air contained in the heated glass expands and the glass rises very, very slightly above the board. It can slide toward the bottom without any resistance (something to stop it).

Beware of air expansion!
On any aerosol spray can you will find this warning: "Keep out of direct sunlight. Do not expose to temperatures above 50°C (120°F)." After the experiments on these pages, you can understand the reason for these words. The gas compressed in the can that makes the product spray is like air—if it heats up, it will expand and make the aerosol can explode!

When it is hot, air spreads out and occupies more space than when it is cold.

Does air weigh the same cold as when it is hot?

THE SPIRAL

You need:
- square of paper (at least 13 cm [5 in.] on each side)
- pencil
- scissors
- piece of string, about 20 cm (8 in.) long
- source of heat, such as a very hot radiator—or you can use an electric pan under the supervision of an adult

What to do:

1 Draw a spiral on the paper as shown in the picture. Cut along the spiral lines.

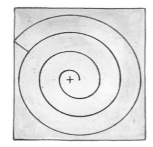

2 Make a little hole in the center of the spiral. Thread the string through and fasten with a knot.

3 Have an adult help you hang the spiral above the source of heat.

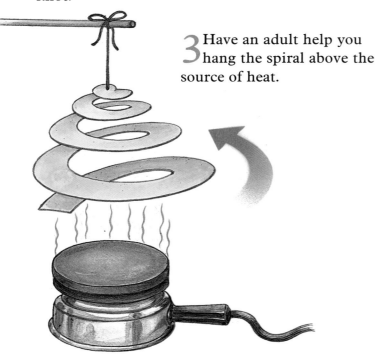

What happens?
The spiral begins to spin around on its own.

Why?
The air is warmed up by the source of heat, and it rises. As it comes in contact with the spiral, the air is channeled between the strips, pressing against them and making the spiral spin around.

Hot air for flying

The hot air inside a hot-air balloon is less dense than the colder air of the atmosphere. So the balloon will remain in flight for as long as the air inside it is heated. The first people to invent a method of rising up in the sky using hot air were two Frenchmen, brothers Etienne and Joseph Montgolfier. In the eighteenth century, they built their first models from paper, heating the air inside by burning straw. In 1783 two other Frenchmen, Jean-François Pilâtre de Rozier and the Marquis d'Arlandes, became the first to travel in a hot-air balloon built by the Montgolfiers.

Free flight

The flight of sailplanes (aircraft without engines) is called gliding. This is made possible by the presence in the atmosphere of thermals—currents of hot air that rise up faster than the sailplane, or glider, can descend.

After being towed into the air by an aircraft with an engine, the glider rises on a spiral path by using a thermal, then proceeds to glide in free flight until it meets another thermal. The skill of the pilot is knowing exactly the conditions in which these thermals form and change. The pilot must steer the glider in such a way that it is possible to find another thermal for the glider to use, so it can continue to fly.

This type of flying is sometimes called thermal soaring because it uses air thermals.

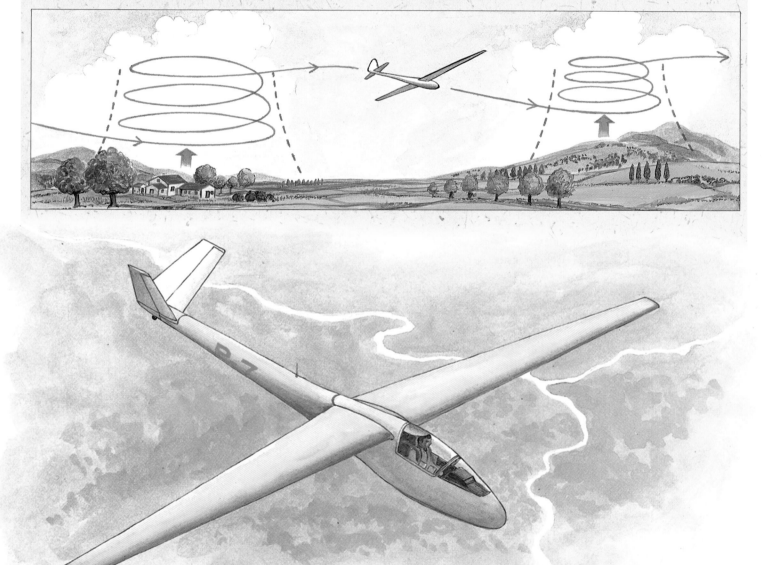

Hot air is lighter than cold air, so it rises.

How does heat spread in the air?

THE CIRCULATION OF AIR

You need:
- tissue paper
- scissors
- string
- tape

This experiment must be done in a warm room in winter.

What to do:

1 Use the tape to stick strips of tissue paper to a piece of string at least 1 meter (3 ft.) long.

2 With another two pieces of tape, stick the ends of the string to the lower corners of a casement window, as shown in the picture.

3 Open the window just enough to pull the string tight. Watch the movement of the tissue-paper strips.

What happens?
The strips bend toward the inside of the room.

Why?
The cold air that enters pushes them.

4 Now repeat the experiment, this time fastening the ends of the string to the top corners of the window.

What happens?
The strips bend toward the outside.

Why?
As cold air comes in below, hot air from the top part of the room escapes, bending the strips as it does so.

Heating up a room

Heat can move through a room. A hot radiator warms the air around it. As the hot air rises, its place is taken by cold air, which is heavier. This air in turn is warmed up and rises. When air is high up, it comes in contact with the ceiling, which is colder, and warms it up. As the hot air loses heat to the other materials, it becomes cold again and descends, and this hot air–cold air–hot air cycle continues. This movement of air from the bottom to the top and from the top to the bottom is called convection.

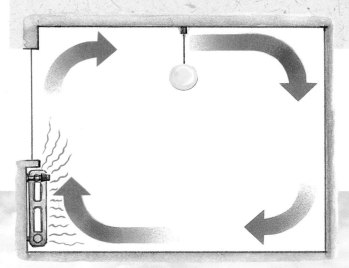

TEST TO CONSERVE HEAT

You need:
- three glass jars with lids
- something made of wool
- sheets of newspaper
- box as deep as the jars
- hot water
- thermometer that can be used in water

What to do:

1 Wrap the first jar in the wool material. Put the second jar in the box and pack crumpled-up newspaper all around it. Leave the third jar uncovered.

2 Fill all three jars with hot water. Take the temperature of each and screw the lids on top.

3 Place the jars somewhere cold (for example, on a balcony or in a cold room) for 30 minutes.

4 Use the thermometer to check which jars of water have cooled the least.

What happens?
The water that cooled the most was in the jar that was uncovered. The water in the jar inside the box with the crumpled-up newspapers and in the jar wrapped in wool material cooled less.

Why?
More warm air was trapped around those two jars because they were insulated against the cold air. This slowed the cooling of the water.

Conserving heat
There are many good conductors of heat. One such conductor is metal (that is why the metal handles of pots soon get hot). We use double glazing (two layers of glass) in windows to prevent the heat inside a home from escaping. Between the two panes of glass there is a gap that traps air, creating a barrier between the warm air inside and the cold air outside. The fibers of wool clothes, the feathers of birds, and the coats of many animals work in the same way—by trapping warm air. Even snow can work as insulation, protecting animals and seeds from harmful frosts.

In the air, heat is transmitted through rising and falling movements called convection currents.

Do hot air and cold air exert the same pressure?

WHAT IS SQUASHING THE BOTTLE?

You need:
- an empty plastic 1 liter (1 qt.) bottle with its cap
- hot water

What to do:

1 Fill the bottle with hot water.

2 After a few seconds, pour out the water and put the cap on immediately.

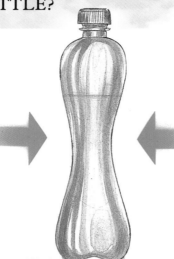

What happens?
You will see the bottle flatten, as if two hands were squeezing it!

Why?
The air inside the bottle is light and expanded because of the heat. Therefore it has a lower pressure than the air on the outside. It is the pressure of the air outside that squashes the bottle.

A view from up high

There are enormous convective currents around Earth, caused by the heat of the Sun. Air continually moves from areas of high pressure, where the air is colder and heavier (as at the north and south poles), to areas of low pressure, where the air is hot and light (as at the equator). The movements of these great masses of air cause winds and changes in temperature. That is why meteorologists and weather forecasters carefully study air masses. In an area of low pressure, we can predict rainy weather because the air rises and water vapor in it condenses to form clouds. In an area of high pressure, dry weather, with clear skies and radiant sunshine, is predicted because the winds push the clouds toward the outside of the area.

A satellite picture of Europe showing swirling air masses over the United Kingdom

Hot air expands and weighs less, and, therefore, exerts a lower pressure than cold air.

How much force does the wind have?

THE THRUST OF WIND

You need:
- piece of thin cardboard
- scissors
- thumbtack
- small stick

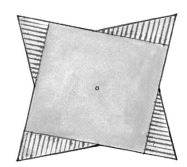

What to do:

1 Cut the cardboard as shown in the picture.

2 Fold the parts that are shaded in the picture to make a pinwheel.

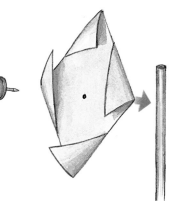

3 Attach the center of the pinwheel to the stick with the thumbtack.

4 Make sure that the pinwheel spins freely. Hold it so the wind catches it.

What happens?
The pinwheel spins fast.

Why?
As the air strikes the cardboard, it is pushed to the sides. But it is stopped at each of the four corners. The thrust of the wind against the four corners pushes the pinwheel around. Windmills and machines on wind farms work in the same way. Wind blows onto the obstacles that can be pushed (for example, sails), making them turn. On wind farms, the energy of the wind is transformed into electrical energy.

Sailboat crews use the energy of the wind to power their boats.

Cyclones

Areas of low pressure are also called cyclonic areas. These areas are more changeable than those of high pressure and can cause cyclones, also called typhoons or hurricanes according to the geographical zone in which they form. Tropical cyclones are the most violent meteorological phenomenon known on Earth. They can create total devastation, destroying everything in their path. In cyclones, the wind spins at speeds that can reach over 500 kilometers [300 mi.] an hour around a central point called the eye of the cyclone. In the eye, the pressure is lower, the sky is clear, and the air is calm.

The wind has great strength. This can be used as a source of energy, but it can also have devastating effects.

Flight

When we see an aircraft taking off, we may wonder how it overcomes the force of gravity, rising up into the sky and flying in the air by means of its strong wings. How are those wings constructed so that they support the great weight of the aircraft? What is the best shape for moving through the air? What features of the air can airplanes make the most use of? What speeds can an aircraft reach?

How does a wing work?

BLOW A SURPRISE

You need:
- strip of paper 10 cm wide and 20 cm long (4 in. × 8 in.)
- sheet of paper
- two thick books

What to do:

1 Hold the sheet of paper under your bottom lip and blow across the top surface.

What happens?
The sheet of paper rises.

Why?
The air that flows across the top surface of the paper exerts a pressure that is less than the pressure underneath, where the air is still. It is the pressure underneath that makes the paper rise.

2 Place the sheet of paper across two books that are set about 10 cm (4 in.) apart. Blow down on the paper.

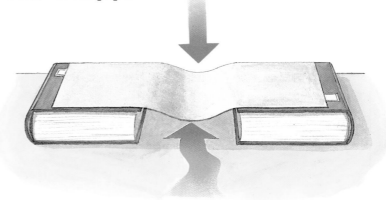

What happens?
The paper sinks down between the books.

Why?
Air is moving underneath the paper, exerting a pressure that is less than that pressing down on the top surface of the paper.

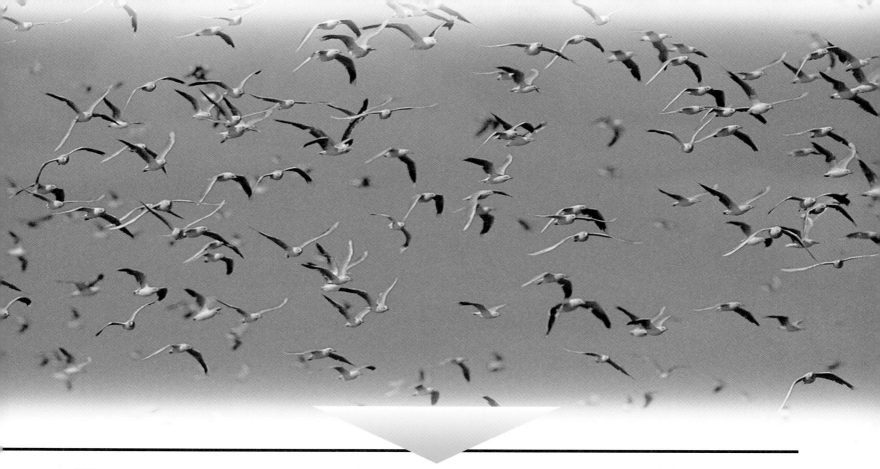

A MAGIC BLOW

You need:
- two balloons
- thread
- drinking straw

What to do:

1 Inflate the balloons and tie a piece of thread around the mouth of each one. Ask someone to hold them by the threads in front of you with a distance of about 30 cm (10 in.) between the two.

2 Blow through the straw so air passes between the balloons.

What happens?
The balloons move closer to one another.

Why?
The air is still around the outside of the two balloons. This still air exerts a greater pressure than the air that flows between them, and so it pushes each balloon toward the other.

Air on the wing

The top surface of a wing is curved and the rear end is lower than the front edge, making the air flow more quickly over the top surface. This means that the pressure of air on the underside of the wing is greater and it pushes the wing upward. The force of this air supports the wing, which means that the airplane is lifted up as the air moves past it. This force is called lift. The flow of air on the wing can be deflected by fins or by control panels called flaps that allow the aircraft to take off, to turn, and to remain at altitude.

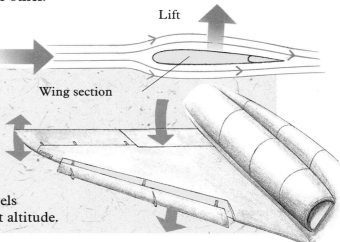

Lift

Wing section

The wing of an aircraft in flight is supported by a force called lift, caused by the air pressure underneath the aircraft.

Which shape is best for flying?

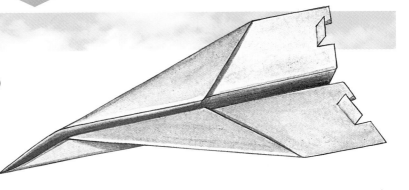

A PAPER AIRPLANE

You need:
- two sheets of 22 cm × 28 cm (8.5 in. × 11 in.) paper

What to do:

1 Make a paper airplane from one sheet, by carefully following the instructions and the drawings below.

 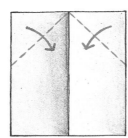 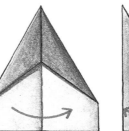  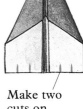

Fold paper along the dotted line, then open it out.

Fold along the dotted lines shown, in the direction of the arrows.

Make two cuts on either side of the center fold.

2 Throw the flat sheet of paper into the air and watch what it does.

3 Throw the paper airplane into the air, and watch what it does.

What happens?
The flat sheet of paper flutters haphazardly in the air and soon falls to the ground. But the paper airplane stays in the air much longer and flies straighter.

Why?
The shape of the paper airplane is made for moving through the air. It uses lift to remain in flight until it uses up the force of the thrust from your hand. The flat sheet gives the air a wide surface to press down on, so it does not fly well.

The wind tunnel

Can you imagine a cube-shaped aircraft? Or a racing car with the front part completely flat? Things that travel at high speeds are built in a shape that reduces the resistance of air to their movement.

A wind tunnel measures and observes objects' aerodynamic features (how well they move through the air). In it, the working model of an aircraft or racing car is kept stationary and subjected to strong currents of air, similar to those it would meet if it were moving. One test is to attach strong threads to the model to show the movement of the air against it. Another test is to treat the model with chemical substances that react by changing color according to temperature. Such procedures, together with special equipment and careful observation by technicians, make it possible to study the force with which the car or aircraft can move through the air (the ratio between its speed and the power necessary for it to move at that speed). The more aerodynamic the

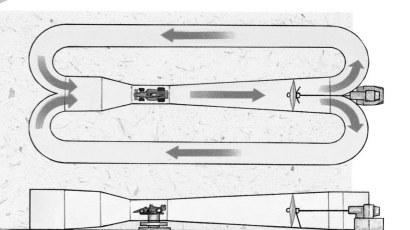

shape is, the less power needed to reach a particular speed. Wind tunnel studies have led to important improvements in the design and building of civil and military aircraft. The straight airplane wing has given way to the delta wing or the variable geometric wing, which can adapt to different speeds. The aerodynamic shape of the fuselage (body of the aircraft) has also become more important.

Supersonic speed

Passenger aircraft fly at an average speed of 800–850 kilometers per hour (km/h) (500–530 mi./h.).

Aircraft that can fly at a speed faster than the speed of sound are called supersonic aircraft. Their speed is measured in Mach numbers. Mach 1 equals the speed of sound, which is about 1050 km/h (653 mi./h.).

The fastest civil aircraft in the world is the Concorde, which flies at a cruising speed of 2,330 km/h (1,450 mi./h.), or Mach 2.2. The fastest military jet aircraft in the world is the Lockheed SR-71 (now retired), which flies at a speed of Mach 3.5.

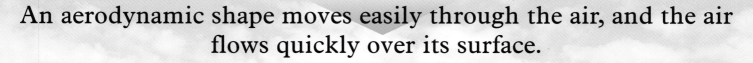

An aerodynamic shape moves easily through the air, and the air flows quickly over its surface.

Air and combustion

It was only at the end of the seventeenth century that scientists found out that air is made up of many gases. By observing a flame burning in a limited amount of air, they discovered the different ways each gas in the air plays its part in the process of combustion (burning). When you light a fire, it will burn more if air is blown onto it. But if you blow too hard on the flame of a candle, it will go out! In these pages you will discover more about the conditions under which things burn, experiment with the features of gases that make up the air, and find out where these gases come from.

What is in the air?

USING UP AIR

You need:
- soup plate
- candle
- clear glass jar that is taller than the candle
- water
- food coloring
- match
- modeling clay

What to do:

1 Use a little clay to hold the candle upright on the plate.

2 Pour a little water into the plate. Add a few drops of food coloring so that the water is easier to see.

3 Ask an adult to light the candle. Then cover it with the glass jar.

What happens?
After a few moments, the flame goes out and the water from the plate rises up into the jar, taking up about a fifth of the space.

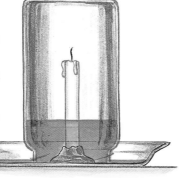

Why?
As the candle burns, it uses up a part of the air called oxygen. The water, pushed up by the pressure of the air outside, enters the jar, taking up the space left by the oxygen. The water cannot fill the jar completely because the rest of the air, which is mostly nitrogen, still takes up space inside.

The components of air
Air consists of oxygen (21%), nitrogen (78%), water vapor, carbon dioxide, and other gases. Nitrogen is an inert (nonreactive) gas that plays no part in the process of combustion.

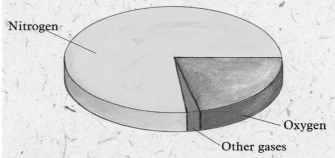

Nitrogen

Oxygen

Other gases

Combustion
Burning is a chemical reaction called combustion. Combustion can happen only with three things present—heat, fuel, and a combustive agent. If one of these is missing, the flame goes out. When we light a candle with a match, we produce the heat necessary for the oxygen (the combustive agent) to burn the wax (fuel) that covers the wick. By blowing out the flame, we take away the heat of the combustive agent, so that combustion stops. This does not happen with a fire in a fireplace because the air that is blown on it cannot take away enough heat to blow it out. Instead, the air feeds the flames with more oxygen, making the fire burn more.

Air is a mixture of gases. Of these, oxygen and nitrogen have the largest share.

How are oxygen and carbon dioxide made?

A PLANT AT WORK

You need:
- few sprigs of a water plant
- bowl
- clear glass jar or vase
- water
- card

What to do:

1 Fill the bowl with water.

2 Place the sprigs in the jar, then fill it with water.

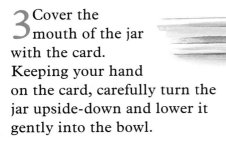

3 Cover the mouth of the jar with the card. Keeping your hand on the card, carefully turn the jar upside-down and lower it gently into the bowl.

4 Place the bowl in sunlight. Carefully remove the card.

What happens?
Little bubbles full of oxygen collect on the leaves. The bubbles rise to the surface.

Why?
The leaves of water plants, just like plants on the ground, release oxygen in the presence of sunlight. Oxygen is invisible, but we can see the leaves releasing it underwater.

Photosynthesis

Green plants are able to make the food they need for growth. They absorb sunlight and carbon dioxide. They use these together with water and chlorophyll (the substance that gives plants their green color) to produce oxygen and glucose, the sugar that is a plant's food. This process is called photosynthesis and happens only during the day. By night, plants absorb oxygen. Without plants, no human or animal life would be possible.

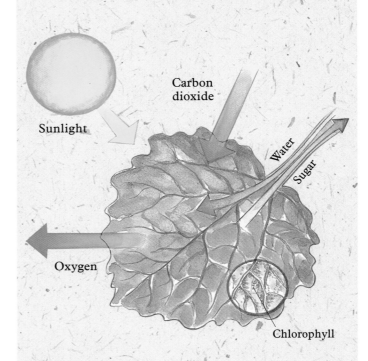

Sunlight

Carbon dioxide

Water

Sugar

Oxygen

Chlorophyll

Why do we breathe?

When we breathe in, we bring air that contains oxygen into our bodies. Our lungs pass the oxygen into our blood, where it is used for the chemical reaction of combustion of food. The waste substance produced by this process is carbon dioxide, which we get rid of when we breathe out. Plants then use carbon dioxide in photosynthesis. We continue to breathe oxygen in and carbon dioxide out for as long as we live.

A CARBON DIOXIDE EXTINGUISHER

You need:
- plate
- drinking glass
- match
- candle
- teaspoon
- vinegar
- sodium bicarbonate (baking soda)
- cardboard tube
- modeling clay

What to do:

1 Use a piece of clay to hold the candle upright on the plate. Ask an adult to light the candle.

2 Hold three fingers against the glass and pour in this measure of vinegar. Add one teaspoon sodium bicarbonate.

3 When bubbles of gas form in the glass, hold one end of the cardboard tube a short distance from the flame (be careful not to hold it too close). Tip the glass slowly against the other end of the tube, as if you were pouring air from the glass into the tube.

What happens?

The flame goes out.

Why?

The bubbles of gas that form when sodium bicarbonate and vinegar are mixed together are carbon dioxide. This gas is heavier than the air, so it goes down the tube and onto the flame, taking away the oxygen. This interrupts the combustion. Fire extinguishers that are used to put out some types of fires, such as those caused by faulty electrical appliances, contain carbon dioxide.

Carbon dioxide in food and drink

The holes we see in some cheeses are caused by carbon dioxide, which develops as milk curdles and becomes sour. The spongy appearance of bread is due to the bubbles of carbon dioxide that develop as yeast makes the dough rise. Carbon dioxide can be used to make drinks fizzy. In its solid state as dry ice, it keeps food and other things cold. If you try putting dry ice in water, you will see it giving off a strange mist and making lots of bubbles.

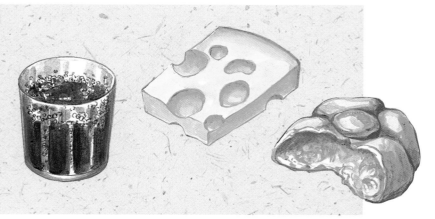

Oxygen is produced by plants. Carbon dioxide is produced when humans and animals exhale.

Sounds

Our life is filled with sounds and noises that help us to understand what is going on around us. The sounds are "decoded" by our brain. Sounds are produced by objects that vibrate. If you place a hand on your throat while you are speaking, you will feel the vibration of your vocal chords. But how can sounds reach our ears? And what is needed to make sounds spread?

How do sounds spread?

SEE SOUND

You need:
- sheet of plastic cut from a plastic bag
- rubber band
- plastic bowl
- saucepan
- wooden mixing spoon
- coarse-grain salt or rice

What to do:

1 Put the plastic sheet over the top of the bowl. Tightly stretch the plastic and keep it in place with the rubber band.

2 Place some salt or rice on the plastic.

3 Hold the saucepan near the plastic bowl (but not close enough to touch) and hit the pan a few times with the wooden spoon.

What happens?
The grains of salt or rice jump around.

Why?
When the saucepan is hit, it makes vibrations. This makes the air around the pan vibrate as well, producing sound waves. When these waves hit the bowl, the bowl vibrates and makes the salt or rice jump.

How do we hear sounds?

The human ear is just the right shape to catch sound waves and carry them to the eardrum. The eardrum is a highly sensitive membrane (thin skin). It vibrates as a sound wave reaches it, and these vibrations pass to the liquid inside the cochlea in the inner ear. From here the sound messages are sent along the auditory nerve to the brain, which then decodes them so we can hear.

SEE VIBRATIONS

You need:
- broom handle
- six table-tennis balls
- six pieces of string, each 50 cm (20 in.) long
- two chairs
- tape

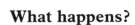

What to do:

1 Place the chairs back to back. Lay the broom handle across the backs of the chairs.

2 Tape a table-tennis ball to the end of each length of string. Then tape the loose end of each piece of string to the broom handle so that each table-tennis ball touches the balls next to it.

3 Pull back the first table-tennis ball so that the string is tightly stretched. Then let go so that the ball hits the next one.

What happens?
All the balls start moving, with the last one in the line swinging as far out as the first.

Why?
The first ball passes the movement to the second, which transmits the movement to the third, and so on. Air molecules that are hit by sound vibrations behave in the same way. Vibrations from an object spread into the air around it. These vibrations are then transmitted from one molecule of air to another.

Sounds spread and reach our ears through air that vibrates.

Are sounds transmitted only through the air?

LIKE A DRUM

You need:
- wristwatch (not digital)
- table
- meter stick or yardstick

What to do:

1 Hold the watch to your ear. Slowly move it away until you can no longer hear it tick. Measure the distance from the watch to your ear.

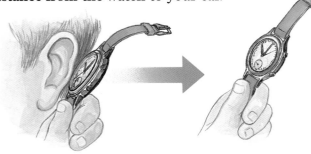

2 Place the watch on the table. Put your ear on the table at the same distance you measured.

What happens?
You can clearly hear the ticking of the watch.

Why?
Sounds are transmitted better through solids than through the air. Sounds travel easily through bricks and glass. That is why sounds can be heard through walls and windows.

Sounds in water

Sounds seem louder underwater. When you swim on your back and your ears are under the surface of the water, your breathing sounds louder. If you hit two stones together in water, you will hear the sound they make very strongly. The speed of sound in water is almost five times faster than it is in air!

At different speeds

In the air, sound travels at 340 meters per second (1,100 ft./sec.). In the same second, sound travels 1,500 meters (4,900 ft.) through water, 5,000 meters (16,400 ft.) through steel, and 4,800 meters (15,700 ft.) through iron. In one second, light travels 300,000 kilometers (186,000 mi.). That is why during a storm we first see lightning and then hear thunder.

Sounds are transmitted through solids and liquids more quickly than through air.

How do string instruments work?

RUBBER BAND SOUNDS

You need:
- aluminum loaf pan
- rubber bands of various thicknesses
- two pens

What to do:

1 Put the rubber bands around the length of the pan about 1 cm (0.5 in.) apart. Try making some sounds by plucking them.

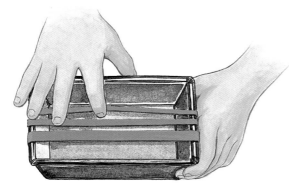

2 Insert the two pens under the rubber bands, one at each end of the pan. Pluck the rubber bands again.

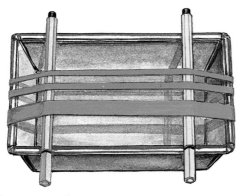

What happens?
When you plucked the rubber bands the first time, the sounds you heard were flat and not very clear. The second time, the sounds were much clearer.

Why?
The first time, the vibrations of the rubber bands were obstructed by the bands rubbing against the edges of the dish. But the pens act like the bridge of a guitar, keeping the rubber bands raised up so they vibrate more easily. The bands resonated the air in the pan, making clearer and deeper sounds. The effect of resonation is also used by instruments such as violins, mandolins, and pianos, all of which have a space that resonates with vibrating sound.

Dangerous resonation

The two prongs of a tuning fork each produce the same note by making the same number of vibrations in the same amount of time. If you were to vibrate only one prong, after a little while the other would also vibrate, struck by vibrations in the air produced by the first prong. The second prong will resonate with the first. Each object has a natural frequency that is set in motion when the object is struck by a sound wave that has the same vibration frequency. A bridge may collapse if the oscillations (vibrations) caused by the wind, or the movement of people and vehicles across it, are equal to the vibrations that the bridge makes on its own. If this happens, all the vibrations resonate together at the same frequency, putting the whole structure in serious danger.

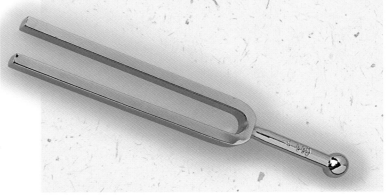

Instruments with strings have a space for resonation, or air vibration, that amplifies sound.

Fact-Finder

Weather stations

Forecasting the changes in weather has always been very important, especially for agriculture, shipping, and aviation. Daily weather predictions are easily available, and people follow forecasts on television and radio to help plan their work and travel. Improving technology makes weather forecasting increasingly more detailed and almost entirely accurate up to five days ahead. This is because there are about nine thousand weather stations all over the world, and approximately eight hundred above Earth's surface. They send and receive data sent from special aircraft and ships, weather balloons, and satellites in space that photograph the movement of masses of air and measure their temperature. This information is then analyzed by special computers that can then forecast possible developments.

The hemispheres of Magdeburg

In the seventeenth century, Otto von Guericke, a physicist from Magdeburg, Germany, used a special pump to remove all the air from a copper container that had been split in two halves. Because there was no air pressure inside the container, the air pressure outside its walls held the two halves together so firmly that eight horses attached to each half could not separate them.

Humans and flight: important stages

1783—in France, the first manned flight, a hot-air balloon with two men on board. Some people call a hot-air balloon a Montgolfier, the name of its inventors.
1852—French aviator Henri Giffard built and piloted a dirigible (airship) powered by a propeller that was activated by a steam engine. A nonrigid airship has a floppy covering that keeps its shape because of the gas (hydrogen or helium) inside it.
1900—German inventor Graf von Zeppelin built the first rigid airship.
1903—in North Carolina, brothers Orville and Wilbur Wright built the first airplane powered by a gasoline engine. It flew for 59 seconds.
1927—American Charles Lindberg completed the first nonstop transatlantic flight in 33 hours and 29 minutes in a single-engine monoplane.
1931—two American pilots, Post and Gatty, completed an around-the-world flight in a single-engine aircraft.
1939—Russian-born engineer Igor Sikorsky designed the first helicopter.
1952—an American military helicopter completed a transatlantic flight in 42 hours.
1957—the military aircraft Boeing B52 completed the first nonstop around-the-world flight in 45 hours and 19 minutes.
1976—supersonic aircraft Concorde, built by the French and the English, flew from London and Paris to Washington, D.C., in 3 hours, 35 minutes.

Torricelli's barometer

In 1643 the Italian scientist Evangelista Torricelli discovered the true meaning of air pressure. He filled a glass tube that was closed at one end with mercury. Then he turned the tube upside-down, closing the other end with his finger, and immersed the tube in a vase with other mercury. When he removed his finger, the mercury rose to 76 cm (30 in.), then stopped. At that moment, the external atmospheric pressure that was pressing on the vase was the same as that inside the tube that held the mercury. Since the weight of 76 cm of mercury was 1.033 kg (2.275 lbs.) and the tube had a base of 1 cm^2 (0.2 sq. in.), Torricelli estimated that the atmosphere exerted a pressure of just over one kilogram for each square centimeter of surface area. The instrument invented by Torricelli to measure air pressure is called a barometer.

Metric Conversion Table

When you know:	Multiply by:	To find:
inches (in.)	2.54	centimeters (cm)
feet (ft.)	0.3048	meters (m)
yards (yd.)	0.9144	meters (m)
miles (mi.)	1.609	kilometers (km)
square feet (sq. ft.)	0.093	square meters (m²)
square miles (sq. mi.)	2.59	square kilometers (km²)
acres	0.405	hectares (ha)
quarts (qt.)	0.946	liters (l)
gallons (gal.)	3.785	liters (l)
ounces (oz.)	28.35	grams (g)
pounds (lb.)	0.454	kilograms (kg)
tons	0.907	metric tons (t)

To convert degrees Fahrenheit (°F) to degrees Celsius (°C), subtract 32, then multiply by $\frac{5}{9}$.

Glossary

aerodynamics: the study of the movement of objects through the air

altimeter: an instrument used to determine height above the ground by measuring changes in atmospheric pressure

atmosphere: the layer of gas that surrounds Earth

atmospheric pressure: the weight of the gas that surrounds Earth and presses down on Earth's surface

barometer: an instrument used to measure atmospheric pressure

combustion: a chemical reaction in which oxygen, fuel, and heat combine to produce burning

compressed air: air that has been reduced in volume by strong outside pressure

conductor of heat: a substance through which heat can flow

convection: the circulation of molecules through a liquid or gas. Warmer liquid or gas rises, and cooler liquid or gas descends.

convection current: hot air or water rising, or cool air or water descending

gravity: the naturally occurring force that attracts objects toward the center of Earth

lift: the force that holds an aircraft up in the air. Lift occurs because the air above the aircraft's wings is lower in pressure than the air under the wings.

molecule: the smallest part of a substance that has all the properties of the substance. A molecule is made up of one or more atoms.

photosynthesis: the process in which green plants use energy from sunlight to make their own food out of carbon dioxide and water

sound: vibrations carried through a substance such as air that can be heard by the ears

tuning fork: an instrument with two metal prongs that makes a certain fixed tone when it is struck

vibration: a rapid back-and-forth motion

weight: the force of gravity acting on an object

wind: a moving mass of air in the atmosphere. Wind is caused by differences in temperature and air pressure.

For Further Reading

Ardley, Neil. *Science Book of Air.* Orlando: Harcourt Brace, 1991.

Asimov, Isaac. *Asimov's Chronology of Science and Discovery.* New York: HarperCollins, 1994.

Fleisher, Paul. *Liquids and Gases.* Minneapolis: Lerner Publications Company, 2002.

———. *Matter and Energy.* Minneapolis: Lerner Publications Company, 2002.

Gardner, Robert. *Science Project Ideas About Air.* Berkeley Heights, NJ: Enslow Publishers, Inc., 1997.

Gore, Gordon R. *Air.* Toronto: Trifolium Books, Inc., 2001.

Johnson, Rebecca L. *Investigating the Ozone Hole.* Minneapolis: Lerner Publications Company, 1993.

Kahl, Jonathan D. *Weatherwise.* Minneapolis: Lerner Publications Company, 1996.

Kerrod, Robin. *Planet Earth.* Minneapolis: Lerner Publications Company, 2000.

Murphy, Bryan. *Experiment with Air.* Minneapolis: Lerner Publications Company, 1992.

Wood, Robert W. *Who?: Famous Experiments for the Young Scientist.* Philadelphia: Chelsea House Publishers, 1999.

Websites

Cool Science, sponsored by the U.S. Department of Energy
<http://www.fetc.doe.gov/coolscience/index.html>

The Franklin Institute Science Museum online
<http://www.fi.edu/tfi/welcome.html>

NPR's *Sounds Like Science* site
<http://www.npr.org/programs/science>

PBS's *A Science Odyssey* site
<http://www.pbs.org/wgbh/aso>

Science Learning Network
<http://www.sln.org>

Science Museum of Minnesota
<http://www.smm.org>

Index

About the Author

Antonella Meiani is an elementary schoolteacher in Milan, Italy. She has written several books and has worked as a consultant for many publishing houses. With this series, she hopes to offer readers the opportunity to have fun with science, to satisfy their curiosity, and to learn essential concepts through the simple joy of experimentation.

Photo Acknowledgments

The photographs in this book are reproduced by permission of: Vergani, A., 5; Cade, P., 6; Pidello, G., 10–11; Ghislandi, R., 13; Wright, G., 16–17; title page Air, Contrast 97; Sappa, C., 18; Archivio IGDA, 22, 34; Quemere, E., 23; Jaccod, P., 24–25; Laura Ronchi, 27; Wysocki, 28; Massey Teatro alla Scala/Lelli-Masotti, 32–33; Dani, © 35. Front cover (top): Jim Koepnick/ Experimental Aircraft Association; front cover (bottom): Todd Strand/Independent Picture Service; back cover: Macon-Bibb County Convention and Visitors Bureau.

Illustrations by Pier Giorgio Citterio.